OIL AND WATER WON'T MIX AND OTHER MIXTURE SEPARATION TECHNIQUES

Chemistry Book for Kids 8-10 | Children's Chemistry Books

Oil on water surface

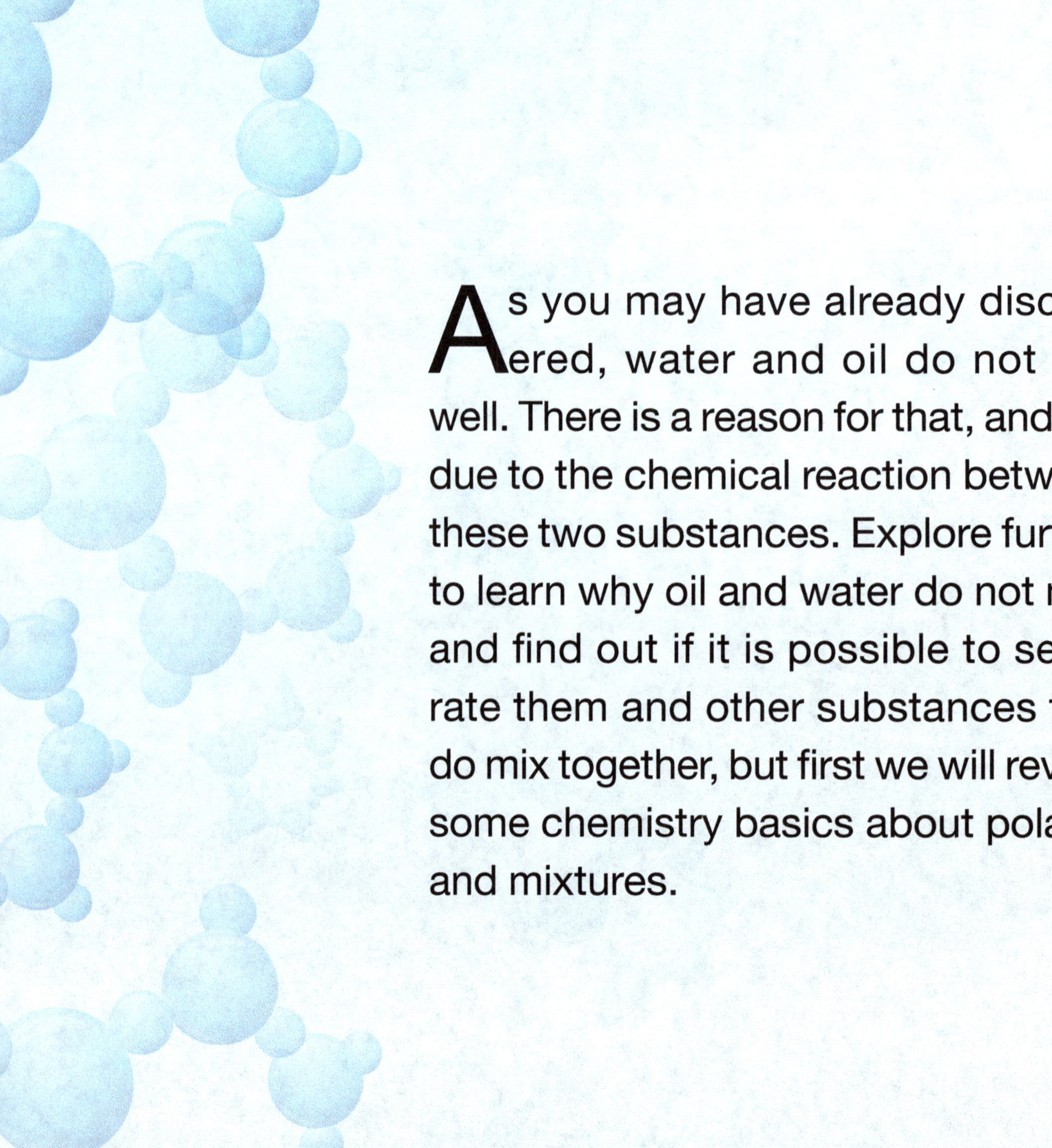

As you may have already discovered, water and oil do not mix well. There is a reason for that, and it is due to the chemical reaction between these two substances. Explore further to learn why oil and water do not mix, and find out if it is possible to separate them and other substances that do mix together, but first we will review some chemistry basics about polarity and mixtures.

Have you noticed that when you have oil on your hands and attempt to wash it off with water only, the water has no effect on the oil that is on your hands? Or, what if a drop of oil is placed into a cup of water, it stays on top of the water rather than mixing with the water? Chemistry! That is why you get this result from mixing water and oil.

POLARITY

Water is considered a polar mole-cule and that is why it does not mix with oil. When one end contains a negative charge and the other end has a positive charge, the end result is polarity. One molecule of water consists of one oxygen atom and two hydrogen atoms, however, these atoms do not form a line. Its two hydrogen atoms hold onto one side of the oxygen atom which makes the molecule appear similar to a Mickey Mouse head.

WATER (H_2O) MOLECULE

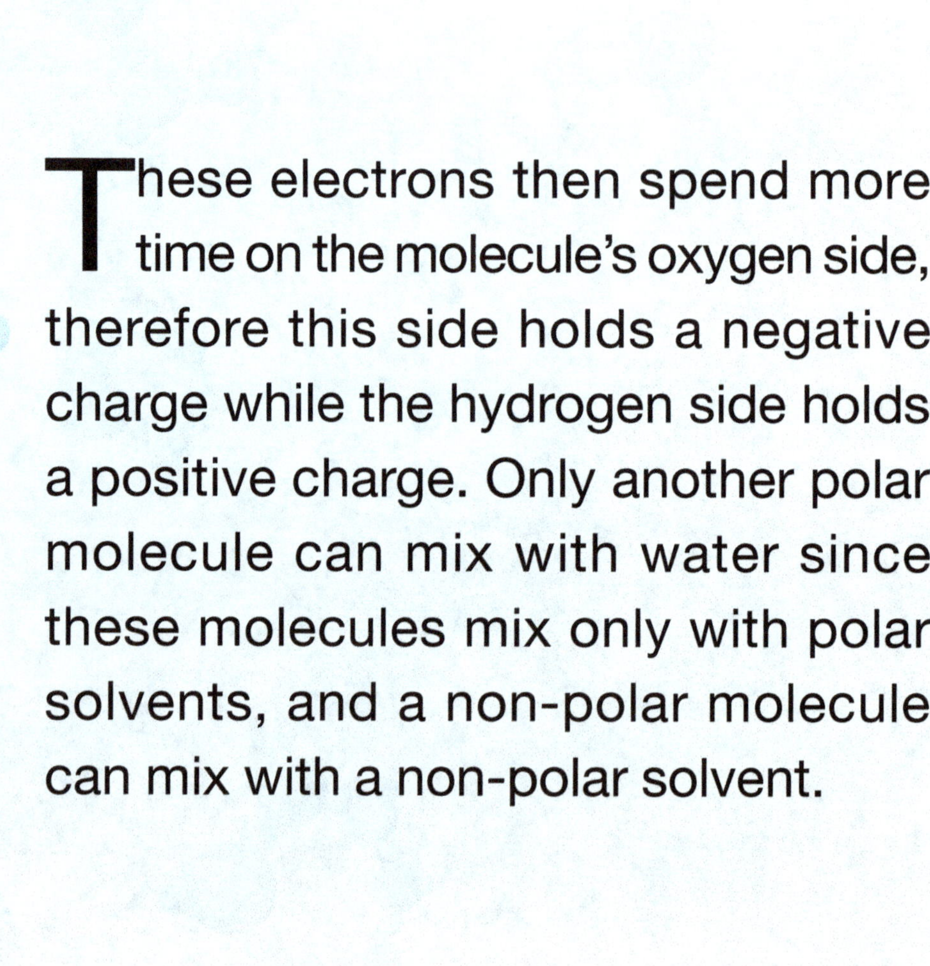

These electrons then spend more time on the molecule's oxygen side, therefore this side holds a negative charge while the hydrogen side holds a positive charge. Only another polar molecule can mix with water since these molecules mix only with polar solvents, and a non-polar molecule can mix with a non-polar solvent.

Due to the fact that oil consists of non-polar molecules and water consists of polar molecules, they will not mix. Since a water molecule is electrically charged, they attract to the other molecules of water and ignore the oil molecules. This will ultimately make the oil molecules, also known as lipids, clump.

MIXTURES

A mixture is the result when two or more substances combine, but not chemically.

General properties of a mixture include: its components can be separated easily, they each retain their original property, and the proportions of each component varies.

Smoke is a mixture of particles which are suspended in air. Tap water is a mix of water and other various particles.

Smoke is a collection of airborne solid and liquid
particulates and gases emitted when a material
undergoes combustion or pyrolysis

TYPES OF MIXTURES

Mixtures fall in two main categories: homogeneous and heterogeneous. A homogenous mixture occurs when all substances are distributed evenly throughout the mixture (Blood, Air, Salt Water). A heterogeneous mixture occurs when the substances are not distributed evenly throughout the mixture (Rocks, Pizza, Chocolate Chip Cookies).

Within the heterogeneous and homogeneous categories, there are more specific types that includes solutions, alloys, suspension, and colloids.

Ocean

SOLUTIONS – HOMOGENEOUS

A solution is comprised of a mixture when one substance dissolves into another. The dissolving substance is referred to as a solute. The non-dissolving substance is referred to as a solvent.

Salt water is a perfect illustration of a solution. Its components have the ability to be separated easily by evaporation, retaining each of their properties in their original state. However, once the salt dissolves in the water and you are not able to see it, it is then distributed evenly into water. In this case, salt is the solute and water is the solvent.

WHAT IS THE DIFFERENCE BETWEEN A SOLUTION AND A MIXTURE?

In the world of chemistry, a solution is essentially a form of mixture that is uniform throughout. Think about the salt water discussed earlier. This is known as a "homogenous mixture." If a mixture is not uniform throughout, it is not a solution. Think about sand in water. This is referred to as a "heterogeneous mixture."

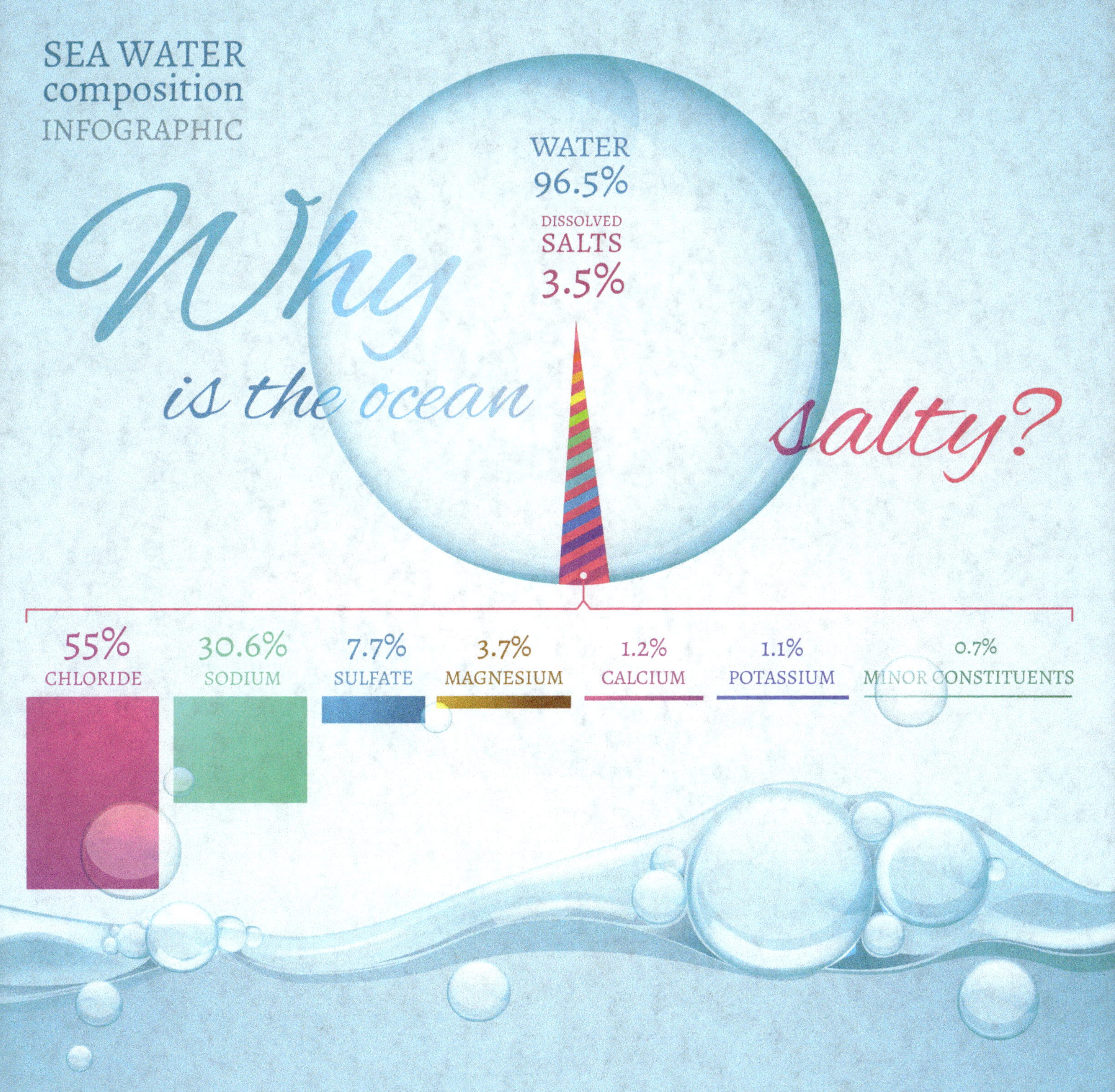

SEA WATER
composition
INFOGRAPHIC
Why
is the ocean
salty?
WATER
96.5%
DISSOLVED
SALTS
3.5%
55%
CHLORIDE
30.6%
SODIUM
7.7%
SULFATE
3.7%
MAGNESIUM
1.2%
CALCIUM
1.1%
POTASSIUM
0.7%
MINOR CONSTITUENTS

Master alloys production from molten aluminium

ALLOYS – HOMOGENOUS

An alloy is comprised of an elements mixture having a metal characteristic and metal has to be one of the mixed elements. Steel is comprised of carbon and iron is a perfect example of any alloy.

Pig iron (grey)- intermediate ore reduction
furnace has a very high carbon content

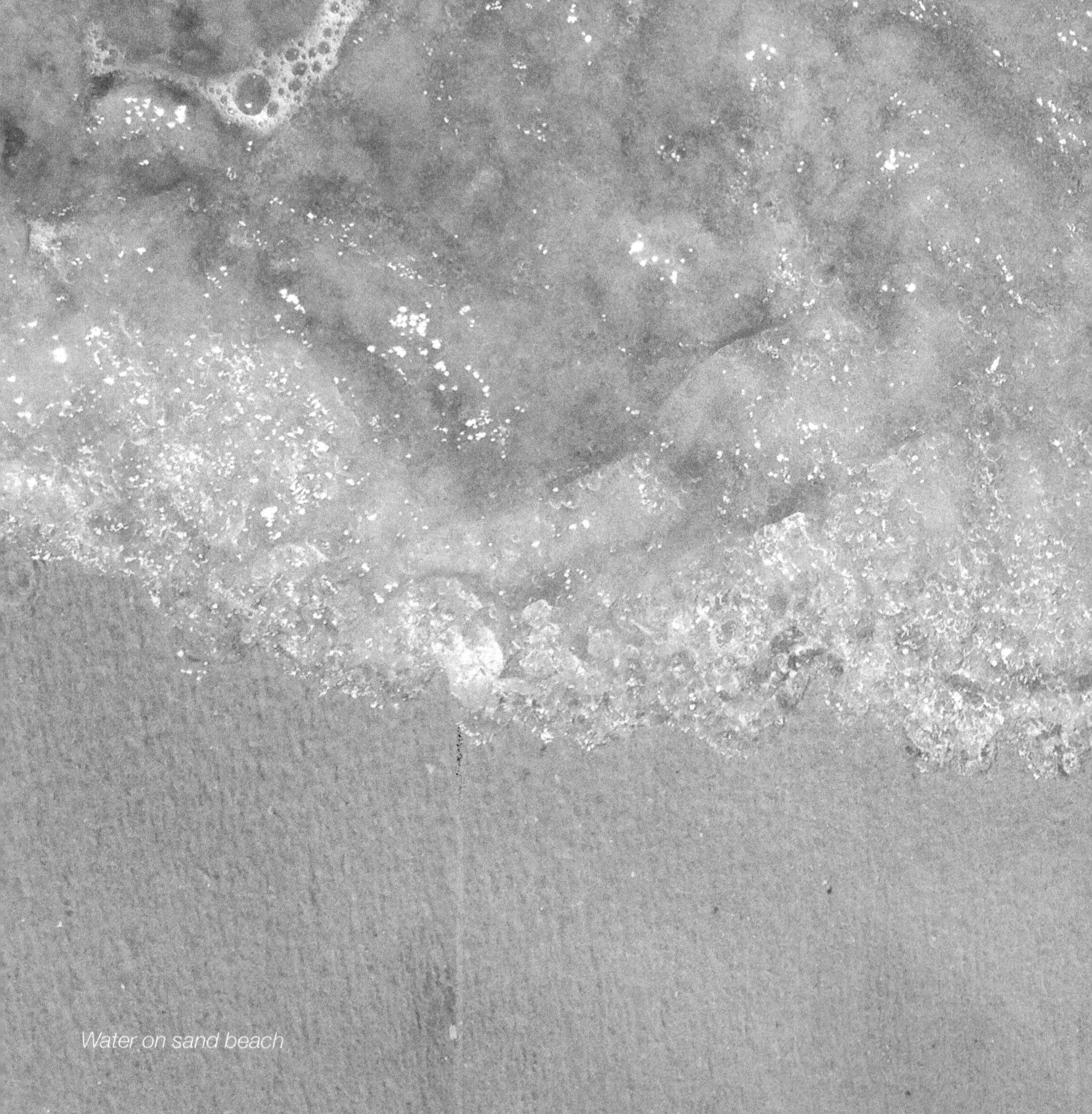

Water on sand beach

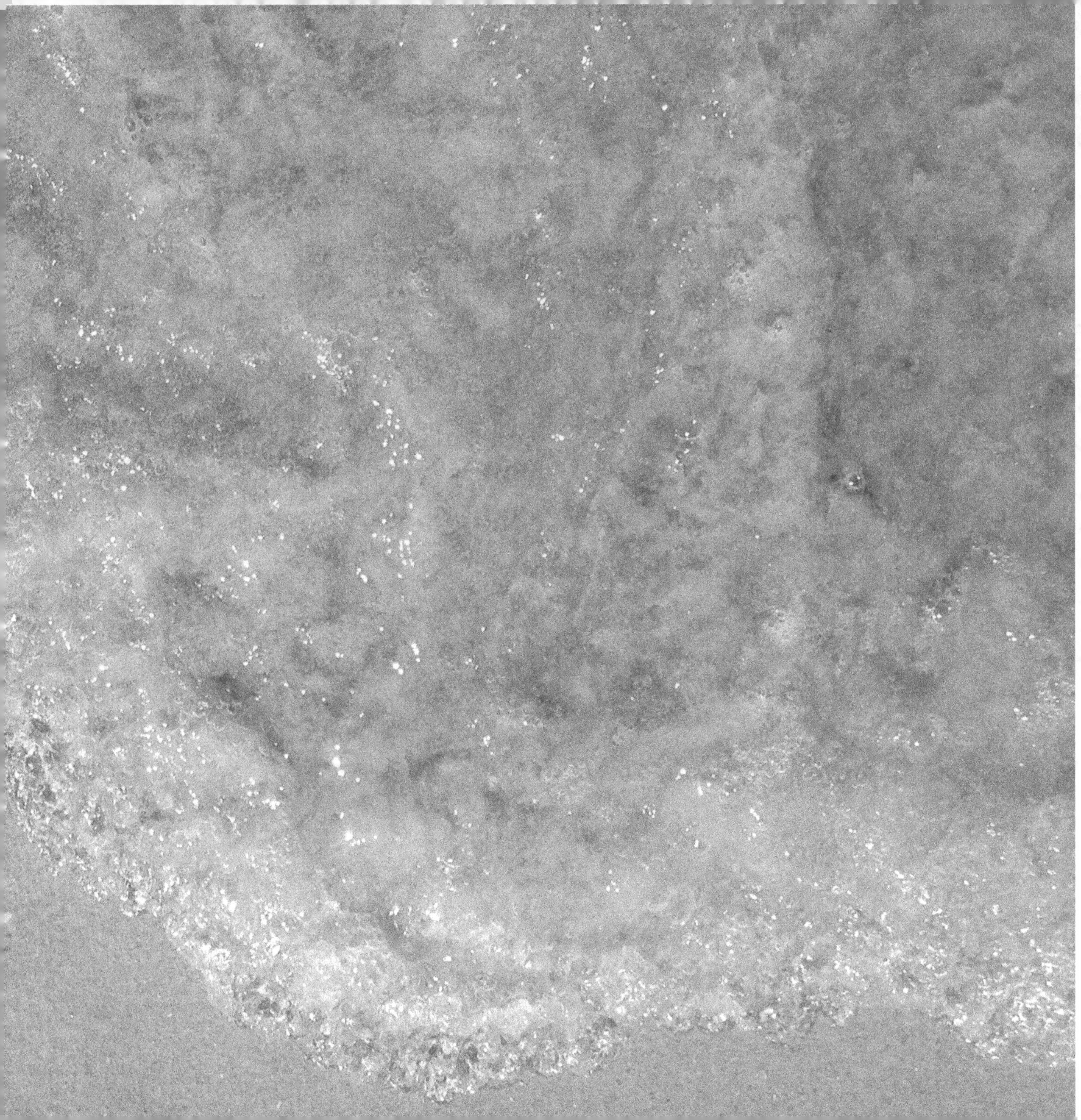

SUSPENSIONS – HETEROGENEOUS

Suspensions consist of a mixture between particles of a solid and a liquid, and its particles will not dissolve. They are mixed and the particles then disperse throughout the liquid. The particles are then "suspended" in the liquid. A suspension characteristic is when the particles settle and over time they will separate when left alone. A mix of sand and water is a perfect example. The sand disperses through the water when mixed, but when left alone it will settle.

Colloidal Pool at Norris Geyser Basin at
Yellowstone National Park, Wyoming, USA

COLLOIDS – HETEROGENEOUS

A colloid is the result when tiny parti-cles of a substance evenly distrib-ute through another substance. They may seem similar to a solution, but its particles remain suspended rather than dissolve in the solution. The difference is that these particles do not settle over time, they remain suspended or they float.

Raw milk poured in pail

Milk is an example of a colloid. It is a mix of globules of liquid butter-fat that have dispersed and remain suspended in the water. They are typically known to be heterogeneous, but may contain homogeneous qualities also.

Raw milk

Salt ponds in Peru

SEPARATING MIXTURES

Many substances used in our everyday life once were some form of a mixture. At some point, somewhere, someone would separate a substance apart from the mixture in order for us to use it. Several elements and compounds are not available in their base form in nature, but found from parts of mixtures. This process is very important in chemistry and industry. There are several separation processes which occur constantly in nature.

WHY SHOULD WE SEPARATE MIXTURES?

Dating back to Ancient History, diligent people separated mixtures so that they could create a substance specific to the need. The process of making weapons and tools by removing metal from ore is one of many examples of separating mixtures.

Iron ore

Woman winnowing rice by using bamboo basketwork

A process for separation used in our ancient cultures for separating grain from chaff was known as winnowing. The mixture would be tossed in the air and the wind would remove the chaff that was lighter by blowing it away, and leave the grain that was heavier.

Woman winnowing rice

Separating a component substances
from liquid mixture in a laboratory

SEPARATION PROCESSES

Process is described as the way which the various substances in the mixtures can be separated. There are several methods that can be used in separation. Most of these are difficult and involve high temperatures or dangerous chemicals. Many industries in today's world rely on the separation process.

Glass bulb on a rotary laboratory evaporator

EVAPORATION

Evaporation is the process used by paints. In its wet state, the paint is a mix of a solvent and color pigment. Once the solvent is dry and has evaporated, just the color pigment remains. Take a look at the walls inside your house – what you see is the color pigment.

Decorator's hand painting wall with roller

FILTRATION

Filtration is more common method of separation. We use filters every-where. They are used in our homes for filtering the mites and dust out of the air so that we breath clean air. They are also used in filtering the impurities from our water. Our kidneys even act as a filter to remove the bad stuff from our blood.

This process is typically for separating a suspension mixture involving solid small particles being suspended in air or liquid. When water is filtered, it is forced through paper consisting of a very fine mesh fiber. Once the water has gone through this filter, it is known as a filtrate. Residue is the particles which are eliminated from the water.

Filtration process in the laboratory

DISTILLATION

Another separation technique used commonly is known as distillation. This process utilizes boiling as a means to separate the mixtures of liquids. The theory here is that different substances in a mixture have different temperatures at which they boil.

Stainless steel distillation machines

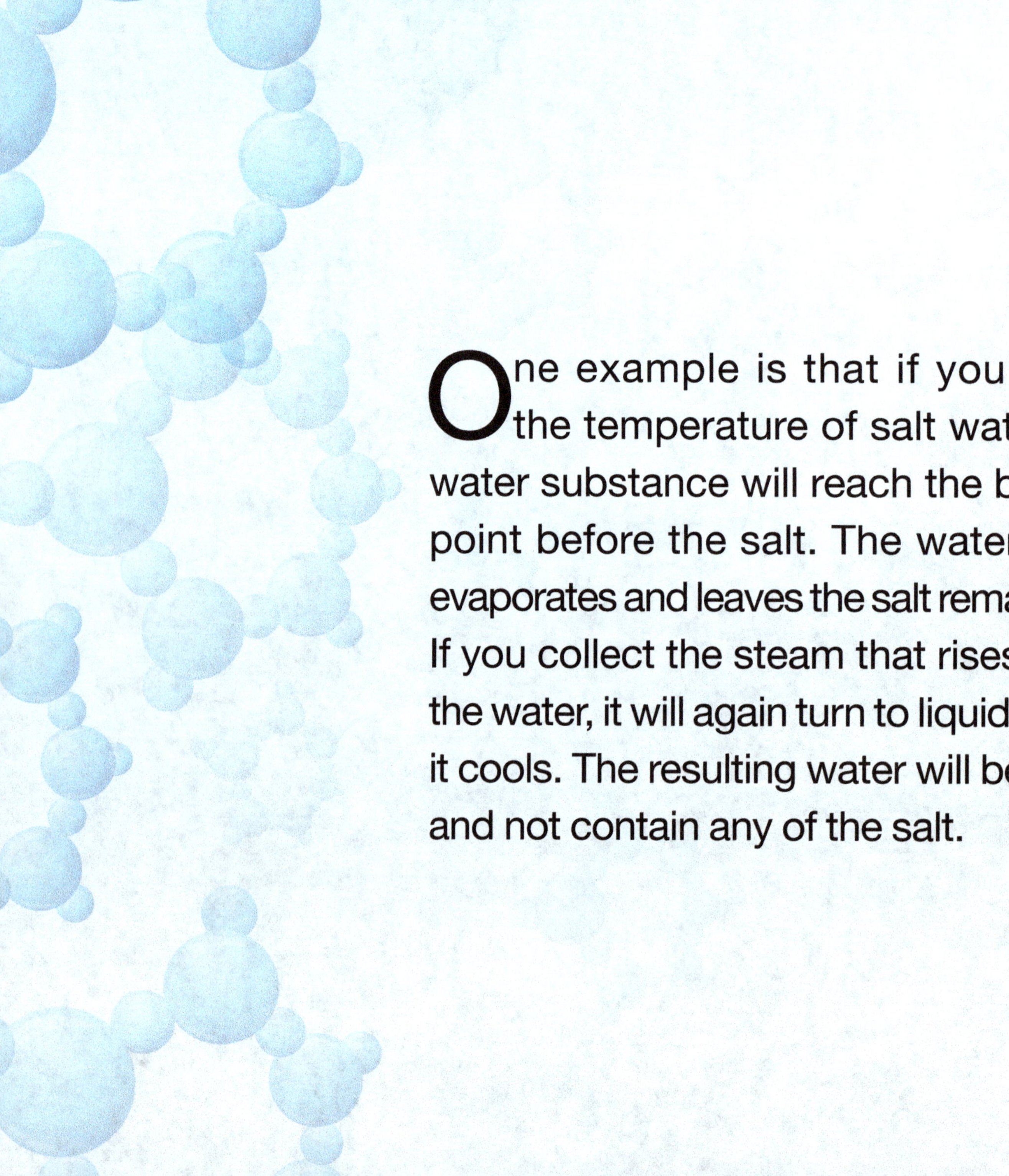

One example is that if you raise the temperature of salt water, its water substance will reach the boiling point before the salt. The water then evaporates and leaves the salt remaining. If you collect the steam that rises from the water, it will again turn to liquid when it cools. The resulting water will be pure and not contain any of the salt.

In order to separate liquid mixtures when the substances might have a similar boiling point, a complex distillation method that is used is called fractional distillation.

Distilled water is water in its pure form, or H_2O.

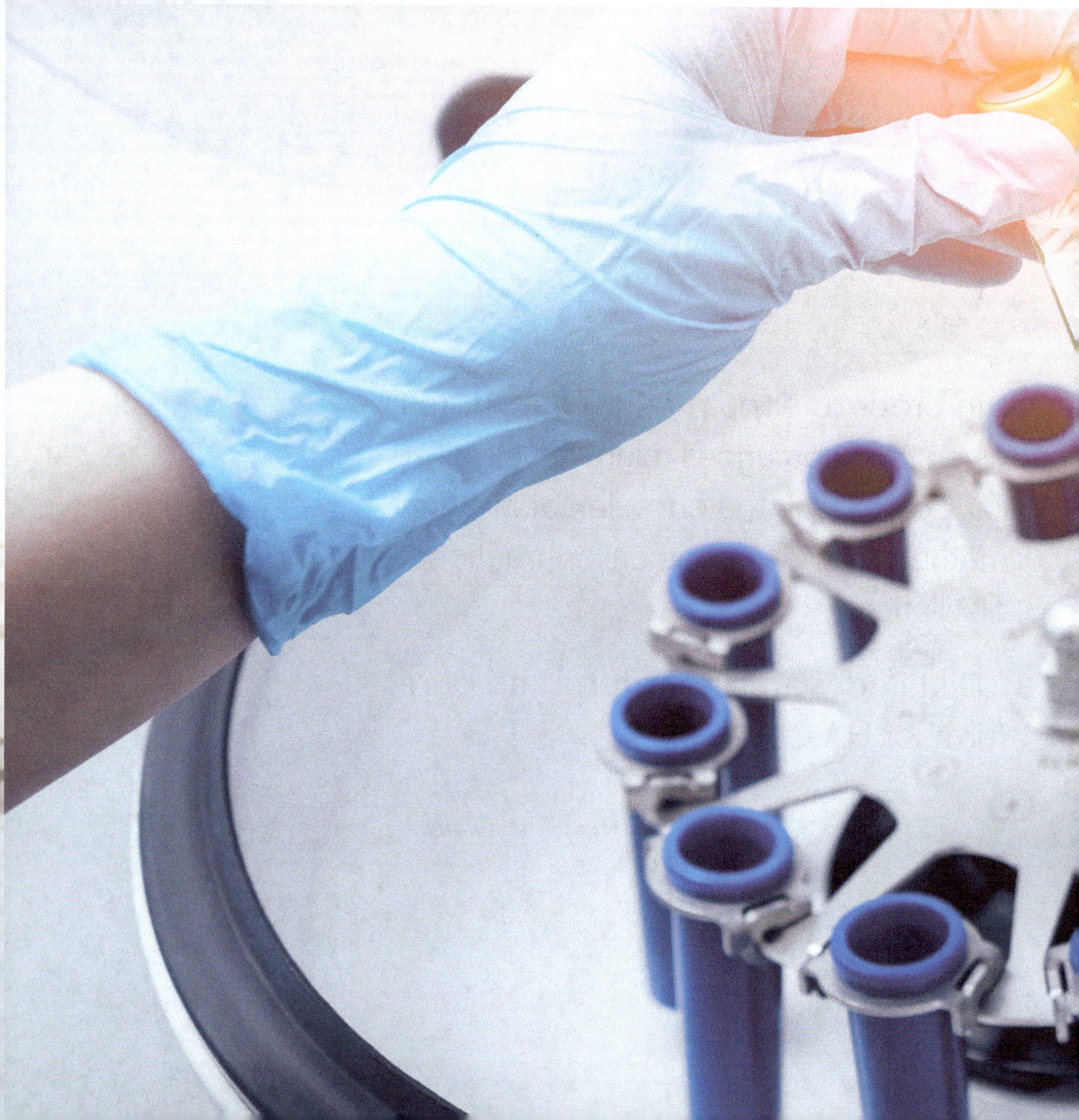

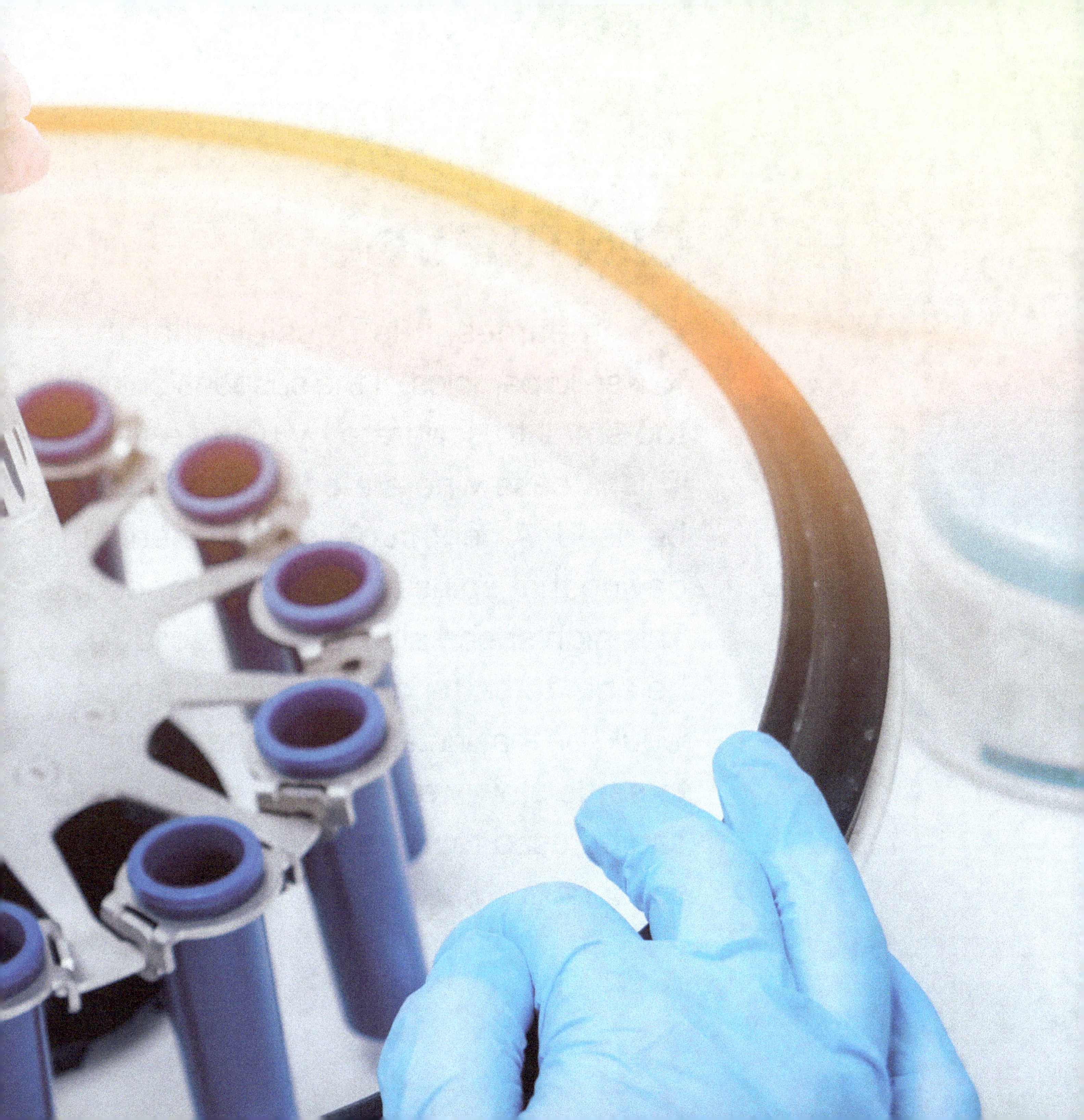

CENTRIFUGE

Sometimes, it is possible that the solid particles of the suspension are too small to separate by using a filter. This is case where a centrifuge might be used. A centrifuge is a mechanical device that spins at a very fast speed. This high speed allows for the solids to be able to settle quickly. An example would be that instead of waiting for sand to settle slowly at the base of water, it can be used to make the sand settle in seconds.

Medical laboratory centrifuge

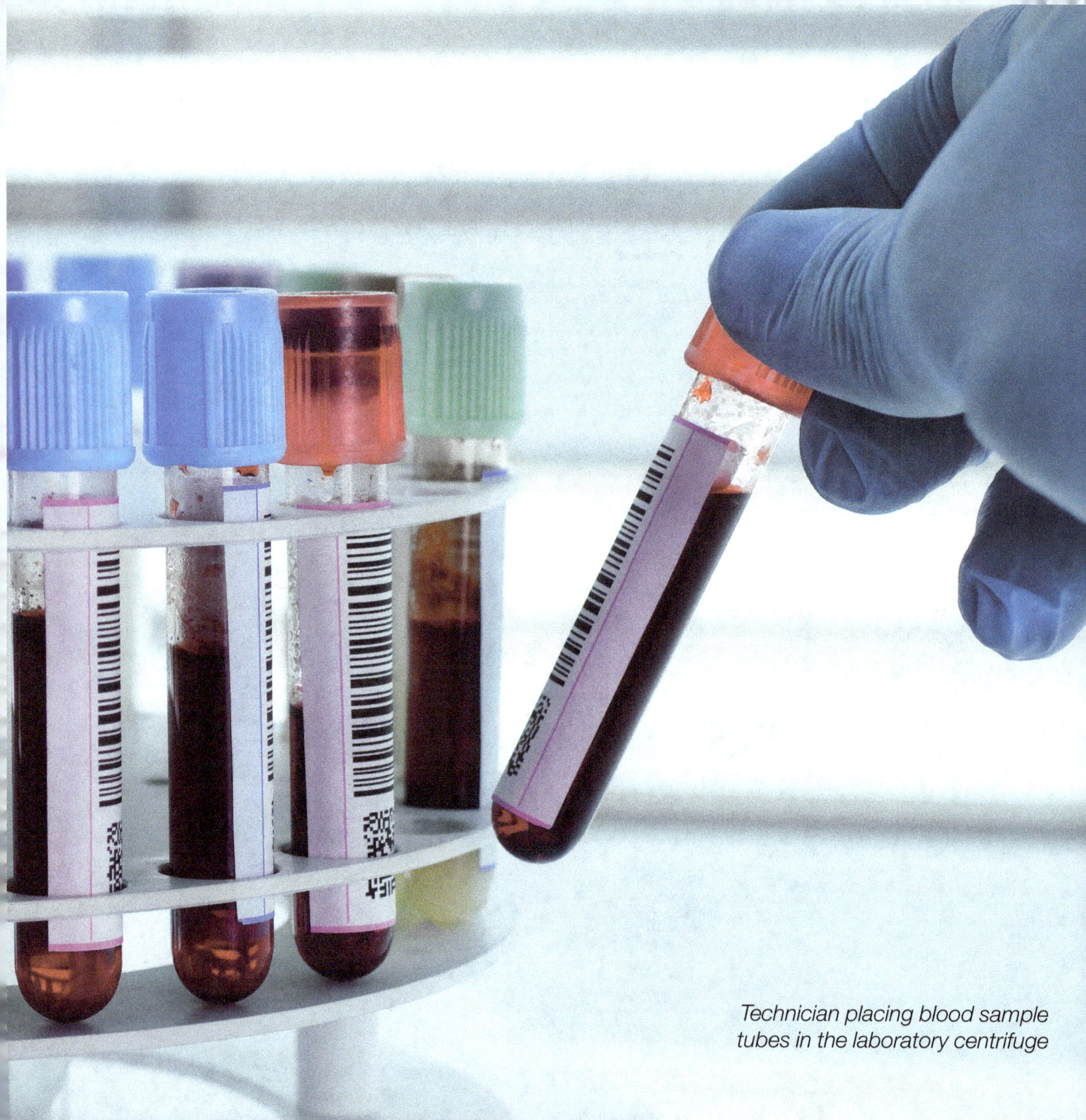

*Technician placing blood sample
tubes in the laboratory centrifuge*

Some circumstances of when a centrifuge might be useful would be to separate blood into red cells and plasma, to separate cream from milk, and to separate uranium isotopes at a nuclear power plant.

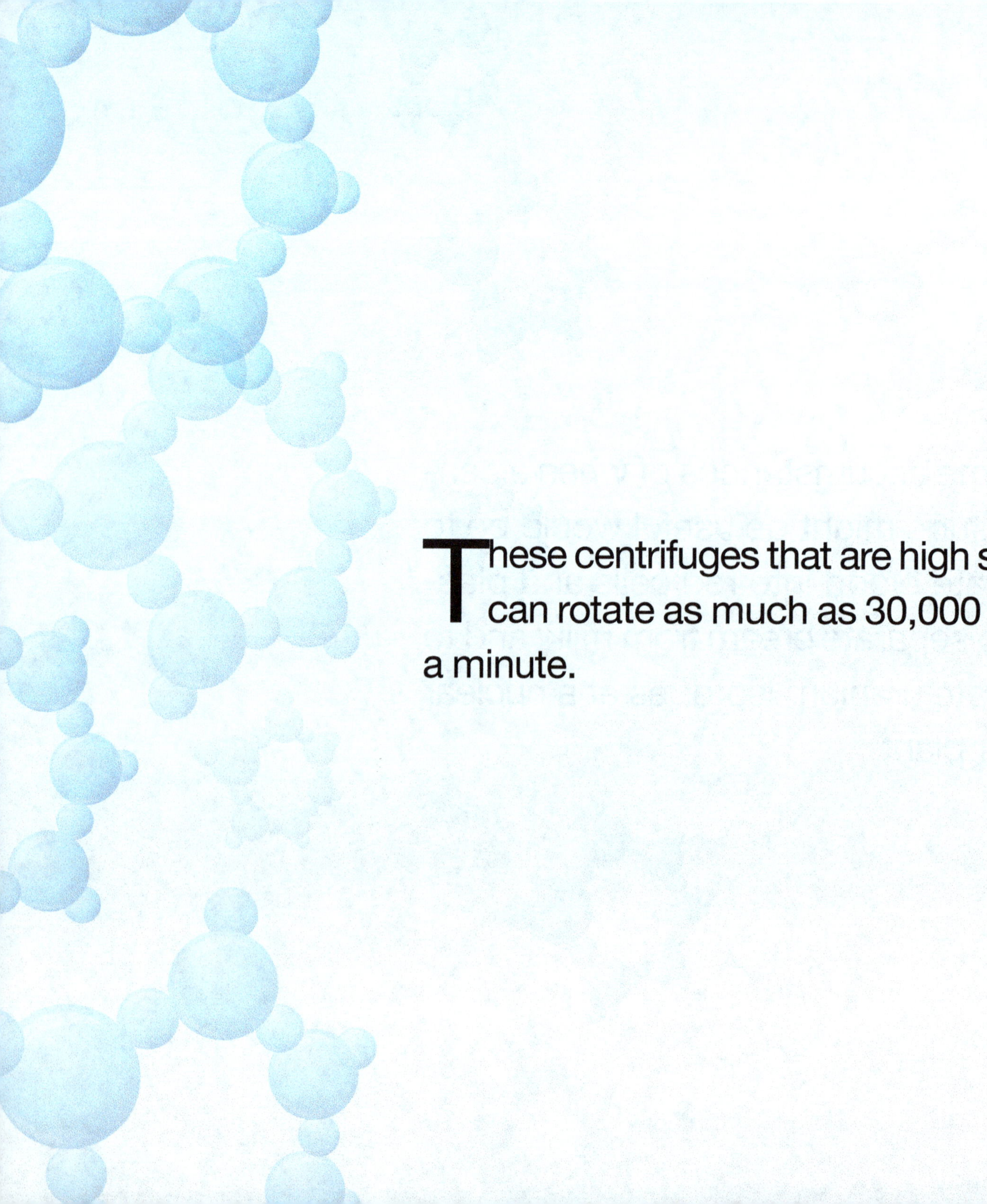

These centrifuges that are high speed can rotate as much as 30,000 times a minute.

For additional information about mixtures, solutions, and how to separate mixtures, research the internet, go to your local library, and ask questions of your teacher, family, and friends

Visit

BABY PROFESSOR
EDUCATION KIDS

www.BabyProfessorBooks.com
to download Free Baby Professor eBooks
and view our catalog of new and exciting
Children's Books